The
Gaiety of Gables

near Reaboro

The Gaiety of Gables

Ontario's Architectural Folk Art

The story of Ontario's Barge Boards,
also called Verge Boards
and by the unversed, *Gingerbread*

"Remember that the most beautiful things in
the world are the most useless:
peacocks and lilies for instance."

John Ruskin: *The Stones of Venice*

Text by
Anthony Adamson

Published by

Photographs by
John Willard

McCLELLAND AND STEWART LIMITED

ISBN 0-7710-0058-8

Illustrated Books Division
McClelland and Stewart Limited
The Canadian Publishers
25 Hollinger Road, Toronto

Printed and bound in Canada

This book is dedicated to a lot of people.

The people whose lawns I've trod and
trees I've climbed.

The people I've almost wiped out on the
highways while looking at houses instead
of the road.

My friends Barry and Dawn Simpson and
Lorne and Deb Lapham who survived
many harrowing U-turns on busy highways.

To Elizabeth Ingolfsrud whose enthusiasm
is as contagious as the common cold.

To Anthony Adamson who had faith
enough in my photographs to write a text.

And to Claire, my wife, who could have
used this book as grounds for divorce,
but didn't.

John Willard

I love old things. Old furniture, old clothing, old cameras and photographs, old dishes, old quilts, old advertising, memorabilia, nostalgia and old houses. Especially old houses. In fact I find it almost impossible to believe that there are people who *don't* like old houses. I, for one, can never resist entering an old abandoned house no matter how many "No Trespassing" signs warn me not to, and some day I may end up in jail. I have even had the nerve to knock on the doors of some occupied houses to see the inside and only once did I get a door slammed in my face. I may have gotten splinters in my nose but it was very good wood from a fine early Canadian door.

Being a photographer, I feel it a mortal sin to leave my house without my camera, especially when heading for a drive into rural areas. Consequently the photographs of old Ontario houses have been piling up over the last four years. Hundreds of these houses are literally dripping with what has come to be known as "Gingerbread", to the bane of many purists. This book is confined to the gable ornamentation referred to by purists as the "barge board". It contains the best variety of examples that I have seen and photographed. There are still a great many I have yet to see and I sincerely regret that the book could not have had at least seven hundred pages to accommodate them all. My apologies to those whose favourite houses could not be included.

Barge boards were not confined to homes. They can be seen also on a number of stores, churches and schools. A really fine village store in Tavistock is trimmed with barge boards, as well as churches in Hagersville, Port Hope and Frome. Schools were not spared a bit of frivolity and a little stone school house at Valens on Highway 97 sports a jaunty cupola with fancy brackets connecting its six pillars . . . not exactly barge boards, but certainly gingerbread.

Alas, I fear that although there may be hundreds of gingerbread houses left in Ontario, they are fast disappearing. Many are being demolished to make way for gas stations and high-rise apartments and other amenities of "Progress". Others are being stripped of their Victorian finery because the owners either can't afford or can't be bothered to keep them up, and still others are being (shudder) modernized. All this is very sad because we are losing a very lovely and amusing form of Canadian folk art. Hence one of the main purposes of this book: to stir an interest and appreciation in our early architecture and to encourage its preservation.

J.W.

near Stratford

Exuberance. This is a word most folk do not apply to Ontarians. But Ontarians once had a folk art which was exuberant, and it blossomed all over the gables and eaves and dripped down over the porches and the verandahs of most of the little vernacular houses of "Canada West" between 1840 and 1870.

This book is about part of this exuberance. It is about barge boards. Many people refer to these lively boards as verge boards, which is certainly more logical because they are boards applied to the verges of gables and eaves. I had always thought with Webster that "verge" had somehow been corrupted to "barge" by some carpenter with a Southern English dialect, but in a glossary of technical terms by Peter Nicholson published in London about 1815 before the Gothic style was revived there is mention only of: "Barge Course: that part of the tiling which projects over the gable of a building and is made up below with mortar." Barge stones are also referred to by other writers as copings to a wall so the word barge must refer to overhang. The Concise Oxford Dictionary says that there was a medieval Latin word "bargus" meaning a gallows. There are therefore two separate and original stem words for the same piece of wood. We may call them by either name. I call them barge boards because I always have, and this is a perfectly good reason.

The barge board came to Ontario with the Gothic revival, but it is late medieval North European in origin. It was particularly popular in fifteenth-century England, and was set up originally in medieval times to cover and preserve the ends of the purlins

or rafter supports which medieval builders used to project out through the walls to support an eaves overhang on the gable roof. These medieval barge boards were morticed into a vertical post at the ridge of the roof called a knop which gave an interesting point or silhouette to the peak of the gable. Some form of protective board at the top of the gable wall to keep the rain and the starlings out is as old as the gable roof itself, but in late Tudor and Jacobean times in Britain these boards were elaborated with hand-chisel carving along their lengths and with pendants at their lower extremities as well as with knops at the top. They were however nearly always good solid boards made of oak and were there for a purpose and not as in Ontario just for the fun of being there and being visible and decorative.

It seems difficult for us today to believe that at the beginning of the nineteenth century Gothic architecture was truly thought even by sophisticates to have been built by Goths. Medieval architecture was a blank page at the end of the seventeenth century in England and it was not until antiquarianism became a popular sport that architects and delineators went out to record old buildings from the Dark Ages and books of drawings were published. These were being published at the same time that new discoveries were being made in Greece and at Graeco-Roman sites. It was all romantically stimulating to a new society growing up in Britain at the beginning of the Industrial Age. In 1791, Sir William Chambers expressed the hope that "even men of inferior rank will now aspire to taste in the fine arts." He hoped they would learn to develop sensitivity to the classical proportions. Instead, in the words of possibly the greatest living British architectural historian Sir John Summerson, "the men of inferior rank established standards of their own, standards confused and debilitated by the literary antiquarianism which in Regency England marched in step with the sentiment of patriotism on the one hand and bourgeois adulation of ancestry on the other . . . . From the bathos of 1830 . . . English architecture . . . slumped into the chaos of incompetence whither the illiterate patronage of the industrial age conducted it."

I don't want to actually say that that is all supercilious nonsense, I just want to think it. But if he is casting aspersions at our Ontario barge boards after 1830, it is my opinion that he is at least in error, even though I know there were others who agreed with him. Augustus Welby Pugin was one. He became the crusader for the revival of the "True Principles of Pointed or Christian Architecture" and he made a lot of scathing remarks in 1841 about what we – and others – were beginning to hang on our gables. He even drew up for ridicule a plate showing what we were doing and then another plate as precept for what we should be doing with barge boards. But we did not do it.

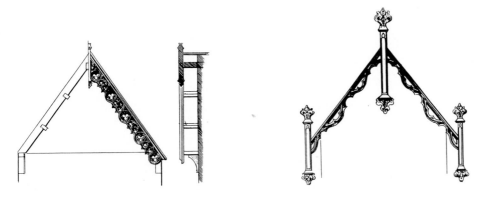

The above is a reproduction from a plate in his *True Principles* showing on the left what a barge board should be, "construction ornamented in an ancient gable"; and on the right what it should not be, but was, on a "Gable in the Villa Gothic Style".

He said our open boards were "utterly useless for the purpose for which they should be fixed, that of covering the timber ends." One of Pugin's troubles was that he was ceaselessly serious. Another was that he did not have the opportunity of working in the finest wood in the world, Ontario's white pine, and the Elizabethans had to use oak because they did not have lots of paint, and anyway we did not push our purlins through the walls to the outside as shown in the section of his "ancient gable" above.

Criticism of so exuberant a folk art as the Ontario barge board is pedantic. No doubt there were excesses carried out in white pine in the 1870's and 1880's. This was largely because an exuberance began at the ground-level in Ontario even before our exuberance got going on the gables. It began first on the verandah posts and when the two exuberances met in the middle of the facade it all became a little heady, more so in the U.S.A. where of course it is always "more so".

The whole history of Canadian architecture is one of digesting influences coming to us from Britain, the U.S.A., and France. In the beginning, in fact up to about 1820, most Ontarians were Americans, either Loyalists and their children or U.S. immigrants who had come North looking for good land. The good land was wild land. Nature was the enemy. The human desires of these pioneers were for a form of shelter which would express the imposition of man's reason and good order upon wilderness nature, and what was a better way than the construction of a rectangular no-nonsense classical or neo-classical building. It was our vernacular style for decades.

No better view of this vernacular style of building exists than that illustrated on the extreme left side of the water-colour of York, Upper Canada, in 1804, painted by Elizabeth Frances Hale. Such simple rectangular buildings were built almost unchanged for the next fifty years.

After the troubles of 1812-1814 and after Napoleon had at last been sent away, permanently this time to Saint Helena, the gates were opened to emigration from the British Isles. In the 1820's and 1830's a quite new social and cultural force appeared in the British North American colonies – a vast number of British immigrants of all classes. They brought with them besides capital and skills some new approaches to architecture. The comfortable vernacular Georgian style was over in Britain and so too was its old philosophic base that there was propriety in repose; Robert Adam had already had his fling with neo-classic elegance.

The two decades following the defeat of Napoleon showed a British architecture in transition, but one in which romance, unrest and a bit of gaiety were quite permissible. There were many fashions and philosophies of art competing for attention in the Regency period but they were all romantic. Meanwhile the second British Empire without its thirteen revolting colonies inexorably expanded around the world. Interestingly, the finest barge boards in the world are Maori, but they were cannibals, pointedly unChristian, and Pugin would not have liked them or their works.

The tear-jerking painting by Ford Maddox Brown entitled "The Last of England", now in the Birmingham Art Gallery, could well be showing an English couple setting out on a five-week Atlantic crossing which will land them up in Canada West. While cabbages for the voyage hang on the rope which separates them from the steerage, somewhere in their portmanteaux are no doubt six crested silver teaspoons and in their hearts a desire to remember "home", the land they loved but had to leave. If they ever got to build themselves a house in their new land what would it be like?

It has never been sufficiently noted in my opinion that the British Empire had a British colonial style. From the Ganges to the Ganaraska there came to be built a one-storey-and-a-half hipped-roofed colonial "cottage" surrounded on two, three or four sides with a verandah. It was never considered a piece of great architecture by its builders. In fact the name it frequently went by, "bungalow", was really a Bengalese word for a light temporary dwelling, what we might have called a "shanty", but it had an overhanging roof supported on posts under which the inhabitants could sit or walk, in the shade or out of the rain. The name for this shady place was not "portico" or "loggia", Italian words used in Georgian times, or "umbrage", an English word, nor was it a word taken from ancient classical times like "stoa" or "peristyle"; it was the East Indian word "verandah". The same word also got into Portuguese.

Upper Canada was a colony. Colonies were hot, but our particular colony was also cold. The emigrating Briton did not look on Ontario emotionally as "home". Home was Britain. But he was happy in his new world with a bungalow – perhaps she was too – and when they found out how rampant flowering vines would grow up their verandah posts, as illustrated below in a house on the Ottawa River, they transformed the posts into trellises. Thus there developed at the ground-level the first of our exuberances – treillage.

The solid rectangular steep-pitched Loyalist classical no-nonsense pre-1812 house might boast a porch in which to doff one's snow shoes.

The still rectangular but larger windowed house with a flatter pitched roof and a pediment on its long side and a little greater elegance inside might in York boast a portico where visitors could fumble for their calling cards.

Quite early inns and a few houses with outlooks had two-storey galleries, but verandahs were not part of the Georgian or Neoclassic tradition. The Loyalist's descendants thought only of Canada as "home". To them there was nothing frivolous about pioneer life nor about the houses they lived in. The well-to-do new immigrants with their crested teaspoons and their new ideas about being British and enjoying life in the colonies were thought eccentric and impractical by the locals. To the new colonists the "Jonathans" were tiresome, but ideas can cross biases and soon the five-window, two-storey conservative Georgian-type vernacular houses grew verandahs, and the verandahs grew treillage, and

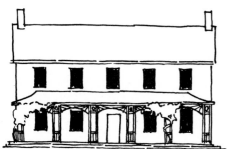

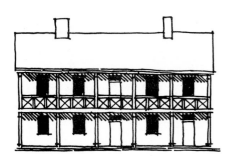

the Loyalists' sons married the colonials' daughters and some lived happily ever after in a new style of house – after 1840 possibly with barge boards, but certainly with a verandah.

The pre-Victorian British colonial cottage was seldom built in Britain although the word bungalow is now part of the suburban vocabulary of those islands. It was built so often in Ontario and so seldom in New York State that it is often referred to as the "Ontario Cottage". It usually grew a tail to house a summer kitchen and its derivative in the 1850's often grew a windowed belvedere from the centre of its roof. The interiors of the Ontario cottage were rather dull, the mantels plain and the trim simple. Its windows looking out into the garden or the landscape or onto the lawns were its chief embellishment, these and the treillage. Much of the latter over the years since its construction has rotted off, and perhaps half the Ontario cottages and early classical houses have lost their wooden verandahs and treillage altogether. In Australia, they built their treillage of cast iron, as they did also to a considerable extent in England where Regency roofed balconies off upstairs drawing rooms came into great demand.

Sydney, N.S.W. 1841   *Toronto, C.W. 1843*

Lower Hutt, N.Z. 1841

At the conclusion of the British Revolution in America there was an American urgency to be un-British. This was heightened in 1812-1814 by the American failure to annex Canada which was thought to be our fault. There was an urgency to create an architecture peculiarly suited to the spirit and the destiny of a society to whom it was self-evident that all white men were created equal. The style of classical architecture known today as American Colonial was at its roots British. Even the Federal style smacked a bit of the Scot Robert Adam, so something else was needed. "Our day of dependence, our long apprenticeship to the learning of other lands draws to a close," wrote Emerson. The old styles were "sere remains of foreign harvests." If England was no longer to be the cultural inspiration, where else to look but to the great treasure house of the ancient classical world. Were not the Greeks and early Romans both republicans and democrats? And was it not also rather romantic to recreate the past? And to recreate the romantic medieval past of Merrie England, was that not a form of cultural subservience? So back to Athens.

There therefore flourished to the South of the Ontario border from 1820 to 1860 a manner which has come to be known as "The Greek Revival". It penetrated to all classes of buildings and to all sections of the country. It was in part a Romantic movement, in part an intellectual exercise in idealism, in part it was chauvinism. But if there was something its buildings had no part of it was barge boards.

The name Greek Revival is in part itself a misnomer; it began as a Roman revival and did not begin in America. Nobody was more Roman in taste than Napoleon. The initial American protagonists of archaeologically correct classical taste were Thomas Jefferson and George Washington, who had every opportunity to turn the course of architecture toward the classics. Education at the time was predominantly a study of Latin and Greek and of ancient classical culture as interpreted through various writings. Both men and women were educated, if they were educated at all, to understand Latin and Greek, so it was very natural that admiration for the latest in ancient architecture and archaeology would have been considerable. The illustration shown above is taken from a most influential American book, *The Modern Builder's Guide* published in 1833 and compiled by Minard Lafever. Such a house was just as romantic a building as the pseudo-medieval castles being built in Britain, but it did have certain drawbacks. Its chief drawback was that a style based on archaeology has a correct basis for its design. There was a correct way to be Greek and an incorrect way to be Greek, and the corollary was that the more exactly Greek the better the architecture. There were few Greek buildings then known which were not temples. This made things a little difficult for the humble folk who wanted to be patriotic and yet live in a house with a summer kitchen and a woodshed. Many a farmer across the border in New York State therefore decked his house with correctly heavy Greek Doric columns up which it was incorrect for trumpet vines to grow.

The advantages which the Ontario cottage and later the other romantic revivals had over the Greek Revival included the ease with which you could tack on a room for grandpaw or for a ciderpress. The Greek Revival was also conceptually rigid, more suited to a Capitol, or a bank, or a mansion, than to the homes of "men of inferior rank". It also suffered from the great disadvantage that at the humble-folk level the local carpenter-builder could not indulge his own creativity. In the later Italianate style he could develop a folk art with ever larger brackets supporting the overhanging eaves. In the Gothic style he could really have fun with barge boards.

The Graecian mode and the accurate Classical Roman "Revival" style lapped over the border into Ontario. There was no iron curtain. In the Niagara peninsula, in settlements along the St. Lawrence, and in isolated towns like Paris, American builder-architects boated across or dropped like parachutists. There the Graecian mode sprang up on houses, but it did not flourish. Into its place, from about 1835, came other romantic "Revival" styles, in particular the Gothic Revival, a style which Sir Kenneth Clark has said was the only purely British-conceived style of architecture in history, and with this style came barge boards, steep gables, irregular plans and the broken silhouette. In Ontario, Greeks and Romans were relegated to County Court houses and places of pomp.

The Ontario cottage or bungalow with verandah was happier on the Ganges than on the Ganaraska in Northumberland County. The shallow hipped roofs, useful as air space in the tropics, were not suitable as bedrooms in Canada. The low-ceilinged upper rooms were hot. Dormers in the roofs spoiled the low ground-hugging self-effacing cottage effect. Belvederes made the structure pretentious. Its plan was rigid. In competition with the Gothic and Italianate Revival the British Colonial and Ontario Cottage lost out.

Ontarians were now in their second and third generation, with their blood lines mixed, proud as punch to be part of an Empire on which the sun never set. Their violent love-hate relationship with their disorderly American erstwhile invaders did nothing to discourage them from looking, as British subjects, to their motherland for a new style of architecture. The same feeling also encouraged them to look askance at the idea of living in classical Yankee temples.

There was of course the little trouble in 1837. If the red-headed emotional demagogue had won, Ontario might have today a lot fewer barge boards than we have, and we might have a lot more farmers living in rotting wooden temples. But Mackenzie did not win and the True Pointed and Christian style did.

The Revival of the True Pointed and Christian style was part of a great romantic movement in literature and the visual arts. It was in part a palliative to the growing urban unease caused by the industrial revolution in Britain. There had been Romantics, of whom Horace Walpole was the most influential, who had built pseudo-medieval, proto-Disneyland cottages and even mansions as early as 1750. Such a building was Fonthill, shown above. This enormous house was a great sensation, and a Canadian, Thomas Ridout of York, gentleman and architect, went specially to England to see it. Robert Adam had built great neo-castles, but with neo-classic interiors. Batty Langley in 1747, John Plaw in 1785, Robert Luger in 1805, Papworth in 1818, P. F. Robinson in 1822, A. W. Pugin in 1836, F. C. Loudon in 1839 and others all started writing books on the joys and proprieties of building houses and castles in medieval as well as in other romantic styles. They were all British.

In Britain, medieval vernacular building crafts had perhaps never died. Much the same sort of hand tools in use in 1450 was in use in 1750 or even 1800. A small rural cottage of 1450 was not dissimilar to a small rural cottage in the outlying parts of Britain in 1750, and all this despite the Renaissance, Brunelleschi Palladio, Mansart and Christopher Wren. The gradual feeding of archaeology into the classical stream made the idea of the revival of medieval architecture less faddish than had at first appeared when Horace Walpole Gothicized his Georgian house Strawberry Hill. Lingering building traditions and crafts in Britain made the revival of Gothic buildings easier. In Quebec, medieval vernacular crafts and even the late medieval style had never died but in the remaining British North American colonies it had never started. But it was not difficult to start.

John Ewart, architect, late of Scotland, now of Toronto, designed a castle in London, Ontario for use as a Court house in 1827-31. This building is illustrated above as it was when first built. Mrs. Anna Jamieson who disliked almost everything there was to dislike in Upper Canada at the time had some praise for this building. It may have had for her certain literary associations or it may have reminded her of back home. In 1827 in Upper Canada it was an exceptionally modern building and I can't help but feel that John Ewart must have enjoyed the idea of building a Tower of London on a River Thames when all around was stumps.

The great excitement in domestic architecture of the 1830's was Sir Alan MacNab's "Dundurn" in Hamilton designed by Robert Wetherell, architect, late of England, now of Hamilton, Upper Canada. It was begun in 1834 and is therefore the first building built in the Italian Villa style in North America. It was even more modern than the London Court house, for castles had been built by Robert Adam and others decades earlier. The Italianate style which got many names such as Tuscan and Bracketed, and the style of which Dundurn is the germinal example on this continent was becoming the most popular style for American domestic architecture at the time of the Civil War. Queen Victoria was to honour the style in 1846 at "Osborne". No American author on the Italianate or Bracketed style that I have read mentions Dundurn nor any British author either.

The romance of Italian houses with towers, stuccoed, round arched, irregular in plan, had been brought back in the mind's eye of those who had made the Grand Tour. Farm houses in Tuscany had towers in which elderly aunts with good eyesight might sit and look out for Barbary Pirates or cattle rustlers. Although the U.S. Marines had tried to get over the sand bar across Hamilton Bay and assault the site of Dundurn in 1813, by 1835 the U.S. Marines were in the Halls of Montezuma or chasing Barbary Pirates themselves off the shores of Tripoli. William Lyon Mackenzie's navy was sunk by Sir Allan above Niagara Falls, so Miss Sophie, the future Countess, could ring for tea in the tower room of Dundurn and Sir Allan could pace his roof and watch his railway.

The most massive romantic influence on Ontario architecture came however from the Church of England which had come with Pugin to realize that Gothic architecture was Christian and that Classical architecture was pagan. This could not have hit the good Anglicans of Hamilton at a worse time than it did because the paint was scarcely dry on what was the finest wooden neo-classic church in Upper Canada before they started pulling it down at the East end to begin building a Gothic brick one. The Gothic style became correct for gradually more and more Christian denominations, but barge boards never appealed to ecclesiologists.

Gothic architecture in its reviving forms in Britain had come to be recognized not only as pleasing, suitable, picturesque, and Christian but also as a national style. Chauvinism dictated in 1835 that the style for the new national Houses of Parliament in London should be Gothic, and somewhere sometime about this date or earlier, someone, an English architect no doubt, put the first barge board on an Ontario house. Wherever it was it is pretty certain that it was a staid board with some carved Gothic lineal decoration on it.

In the nineteenth century whenever an important thought was expressed or treatise written in English it was written by an Englishman or an American. Nineteenth-century Anglophone Canada was bombarded by architectural ideas from two cultures by authors and professors and architects who knew little about Ontario. And yet when all the books on architecture get onto microfilm and all the ideas are fed into computers, Ontario will have left standing at least two of the finest Gothic Revival buildings in the world: the Library of the Parliament Buildings in Ottawa and University College in Toronto; and international scholars will have to punch a lot of U.S. I.B.M. buttons to find any references to them whatever.

St. George's,
Kingston   *St. James', Toronto*

True Pointed and Christian style
defeats the pagans

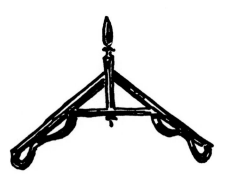

This book is not about great buildings, it is about a vernacular folk art which came along with our British inheritance. We are told by contemporary art and architectural historians that we got this folk art via books published in the U.S.A., derivatives from earlier British authors. The most influential of these U.S. writers was Andrew Jackson Downing (1815-1852).

Downing was a landscape gardener turned "architectural composer". He wrote several books, of which the best known are *Practical Landscape Gardening* – 15 editions, *Cottage Residences* – 5 editions, *Architecture of Country Houses* – 9 editions. These were written between 1841 and 1850. About them Professor Tatum, the editor of the latest edition of Downing's work on country houses, has said: "Taken as a group these four books would seem to have been by far the most popular and influential writings of their kind ever published in America." Downing is credited with being largely responsible for gradually discrediting the Greek Revival as a national American style before its final demise in the Civil War when the word "sublime" sadly vanished from the vocabulary of artists, architects and Americans. Two of his houses are illustrated below, one with barge boards, one with brackets.

On the right, a villa in the Italian style, bracketed. "It is highly irregular," Downing wrote in *Cottage Residence*, "while it will, on account of the greater picturesqueness and variety growing out of this circumstance, be more pleasing to a portion of our readers. A great number of persons, who only judge of a dwelling-house by a common-sense standard, will probably prefer a more regular and uniform building." On the left, a small cottage or gate lodge, which would "make a neat and picturesque dwelling, if properly located, for a small, respectable family, who wish to lead a quiet and simple life."

Downing appealed directly to owners and he had the good fortune to obtain the collaboration of Alexander Jackson Davis (1803-1892), an architect and brilliant delineator. His works would not have been so effective had British copy or source books not preceded him. Nor would American society have been so ready for readable books like his had the Americans Minard Lafever (1798-1854) and the prolific Asher Benjamin (1773-1845) not published before him also. The latter authors were however far from favouring medieval revivals in contrast to Downing who was.

A comparison of John Claudius Loudon's small print, immense technological detail and insignificant architectural drawings on which Downing drew so profusely, show why Downing's books lay on the round tables under the Argand lamps of the best villa parlours in the U.S.A. and the best drawing rooms in Canada and why Loudon's *Encyclopaedia* sat on shelves, for useful reference on almost everything. He even invented the coat hanger in the 1840's. There was nothing he did not appear to know.

For the intellectuals in both countries there were the writings of John Ruskin (1819-1900) as well as A. Welby Pugin (1812-1852). For the Britishers in Canada who might mistrust the Yankee ideas of Downing, yet be interested in romantic architecture, there were the slightly earlier books, starting in 1822, of P. F. Robinson as well as those of E. B. Lamb and Francis Goodwin. These and other books lay not only on the green cloths of the parlour tables, but were lodged in the Mechanics Institutes of the towns and cities of Upper Canada and Canada West. A few finally rest in the public libraries of Ontario. The illustration below shows a "thatched cottage suitable for the Superintendent of an estate" reduced from P. F. Robinson's *Rural Architecture*, 1829, for illustration in Loudon's *Suburban Gardener*.

But what did they all say about barge boards? And where did our Ontario carpenter-builders get their ideas for their designs?

All nineteenth century architectural critics expressed similar basic opinions. Architecture had first to be useful. It had also to be beautiful according to some vague canons variously and at length propounded. But it was still not satisfactory unless it was truthful. Truth in architecture was elusive like the Holy Grail in Arthurian Legends. How does the Ontario barge board stand up against Pugin's admonition: "all ornament should consist of enrichment of the essential construction of a building"? It fails utterly. This questing for truth is echoed again and again in books, periodicals and professorial talk. "Construction must be decorated not decoration constructed." "Ornamental wooden verge boards on brick and stone houses are offensive to the enlightened."

Truth in Architecture

Truth had to be sought in materials and colour. Truth had to be expressed in large chimneys if the building was a house, in plainness if the occupants were poor, in rustic strength if they were farmers, and in the truest pointed Gothic style of the thirteenth century if a church congregation had any pretentions to being Christian. I will only quote one excerpt about this truth theory from one writer, Downing. It relates to our subject barge boards. "As part of a well-built villa a verge board is carefully carved in thick solid plank so as to exhibit all the details of outline and tracery boldly to the eye, and so to endure as long as the house itself. Now let this be imitated in a cheap cottage and it is almost always sawn out of thin board so as to have a frippery and 'gingerbread' look which degrades rather than elevates the beauty of the cottage."

The word "gingerbread" has been applied to all the whittling and piercings and carvings and turnings of woodwork on treillage and brackets and barge boards in High Victorian architecture. It seems to have a curious derivation from an Old French word *gingebras* or *gingimbrat* meaning a fancy kind of cookie flavoured with ginger and built up in varied shapes and sometimes gilded. The term came to be applied to ships' carvings. Simultaneously, in my opinion, Anglophones made ginger biscuits or gingerbread cut with moulds into men or funny shapes. The two terms coalesced and came to be applied in derision to the fancier exterior woodwork of North American buildings.

Derision is what all the authoritative, the philosophic, the trained and the aesthetic had for our barge boards. Trained immigrant architects from Britain tried to bring us to truth and beauty. Some of their good truthful boards may be illustrated in this book. Future study may indicate what barge boards were designed by such Ontario architects as J. G. Howard, Thomas Young, William Thomas, George Browne, R. Wetherell, Kivas

Tully, and the Radford brothers, but as we are neither American nor British nor French we have not had the courage to write about the architecture of Canada. To compound our sins our most prolific architectural historian Allan Gowans does not leave a page unturned without pointing out that our buildings are damnably British. What I think is Ontario's prettiest house, Riverest on the Ottawa River at l'Orignal, he calls a "symbol of a British caste system exported verbatim and defiantly maintained." (It just so happens that that particular house was built for an American—but perhaps by an upper-crust mason.) When our buildings are of American derivation, taking one example, they are "a masterpiece—in the fashionable temple house form of the classical revival." In the first editorial of the first issue of *The Canadian Architect and Builder* in 1888, architect James Balfour wrote, "from an architectural point of view our cities and towns must be considered a failure. This is especially true as regards the character of our homes." And this is especially true about what Canadians say about Canada.

So our barge boards, or most of them, are not good architecture, they are untruthful, they are quite inappropriate on many of the buildings they cling to, they are gingerbread, and they represent a caste system. But all this opinionated erudition does not tell us from whence came the imagination of their makers to design them. It does not appear to have come from copy books nor from all the exhorting authors.

I have looked through the books I can readily find which might have been sources for their imagination. P. F. Robinson's *Rural Architecture*, fourth edition, 1837, has the largest relative number of designs of houses with barge boards, nine out of twenty illustrations, but they are all of a cusped Gothic design and nearly all identical. His *Ornamental Villas*, third edition, 1853, has only two designs out of twenty which have barge boards and one is Swiss. A. J. Downing's famous *Cottage Residences*, 1860 edition,

has four houses with barge boards all simple and truthful. J. C. Loudon's *Encyclopaedia*, 1839, has about six, but so small you can scarcely see them. I show a sketch on the previous page from Loudon in the "Swiss mode". Ontario was never very Swiss. The design was by Robinson – perhaps a relation of the Swiss Family.

By the 1850's however the books on house design became physically larger and supplied details. One of the best known, *The Model Architect, Series of Original Designs* by Samuel Sloan, 1853, has some barge board details. Of his house designs about one third are Gothic. The illustration below is the most useful example of a source for a mid-century Ontario carpenter's work that I can find. The British periodical *The Builder* which began in 1843, *The Canadian Farmer* which began in 1864, and *The Canadian Architect and Builder* beginning in 1888 could be searched for sources of inspiration, but it is my belief that many if not most of the designs were happy individualistic creations. One can see regional similarities of board, finial and pendant design obviously arising from the work of individuals rather than from a copy book source, or bought already made by the foot from a mill.

Before considering what is readily known about the Ontario method of making barge boards and the apparent evolution of the gingerbread which eventually gravitated to the peak of the gables, and which can be seen in this book, I must show two illustrations of prefabricated "galvanized iron cottages easy of conveyance and erection" from the catalogue of The International Exhibition of 1862 held in London. Prefabricated houses in iron for the colonies were commonly exported to Australia. Those illustrated above made me feel a little sympathetic with Pugin and Summerson, but the National Capital Commission has preserved a tin house front in Ottawa and has hung it on a wall for the admiration of "men of inferior rank" and the Civil Service.

Ontario barge boards were attached to nailing strips on the underside of the roof boards. Sometimes the overhang of the eaves had a soffit or a board to hide the nailing strips. Sometimes the boards were morticed into finials and ornamental pendants were hung onto the lower ends. Sometimes the boards were themselves a series of cut-out flat pendants. Sometimes the boards were moulded or bevelled, sometimes they were not. Sometimes they had turned wood embellishments. Usually they were open or pierced. They were attached to gables and dormers and porches of both the flat classical and the steep Gothic pitch. Sometimes they travelled along the horizontal eaves to the next gable.

Some of the finest gingerbread is in Russia and the Scandanavian countries, but to the Upper Canadian of this date their residents were foreign and their ideas questionable. In Britain, barge boards through the 1870's and 1880's dwindled into insignificance. Britain never had a superfluity of wood and the curly gables of the Queen Anne style outpaced the French Mansard roofs. The heyday of British barge boards was probably the late 1840's and early 50's when Pugin was attacking them so strongly. In 1867, the *Canada Farmer* began to make house designs for farmers; the caption to the one shown above says "it is thought quite time that our well-to-do farmers should study taste as well as utility."

Inside the attic, the roof rafters were usually stabilized or tied together by "collars" and it became popular in the 1860's and 1870's to have such collars expressed externally and so have the barge boards tied together with an exposed horizontal board. If there was a finial it would often be fitted into this exposed collar. The new horizontal element caused a lot of going on in the peak of the gable above the exposed collar, and builder-designer architects started to concentrate on this area and neglect the rising eaves of the gable. In the 1880's, holes and sunbursts blazed in the triangles at the peaks. With the introduction of the Mansard roof, gables became fewer, but when a Mansard roof had a gable, the main rising eave was curved and the top pitched.

With the rise in the popularity of wooden brackets to support the wide eaves of Italianate houses, brackets occasionally were placed to support the gable eaves of those Gothic-inspired buildings which had barge boards. Once brackets and collars were introduced, the concept of the medieval "hammer beam" roof grew on gables. In the 1880's, two-storey bay windows often ran up into the gables and large brackets now in line with the face of the house held the unsupported corners of the eaves rigid. By this date during the High Victorian style with the French onrush of Mansard roofs, few could say whether the building was Tudor, Swiss, Italian, Tuscan, Bracketed, Third Empire, or Eclectic, and few could tell where the barge board began and where it became something else. This was the true gingerbread, but it is beyond our date, and is best and most prevalently seen in the U.S.A. and Russia.

There is surprisingly little evidence available as yet on how our Ontario barge boards were cut. Occasional advertisements exist showing that certain saw mills had scroll saws, but I have seen no advertisement for a mill which was prepared to design barge boards or sell them by the foot. It is an area unresearched. From the sources I know of I believe that each builder made a sketch of the gable and the type of board and finial he was going to use. Some no doubt copied directly from copy book designs, such as those illustrated. Having decided on what he wanted, the builder proceeded to draw out on a selected board the proposed pattern along the length of the gable's verge, at the peak, and at the junction with the horizontal eaves. If it was to be a pierced board with straight edges a hole would be drilled and a fret saw blade or a jig saw blade would be inserted. In general the fret saw usually refers to a saw used in joinery and operated with a treadle, whereas a jig saw is used on timber. Another word for jig saw is scroll saw. Once inserted in the hole the blade would commence by up and down reciprocating action to cut out along the marked lines leaving the straight edged board with a pierced pattern.

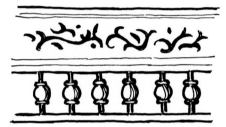

If the board was to have an irregular edge the outer profile would be marked also and the board cut with a band saw in a mill. A band saw is an endless steel belt with teeth at one edge running on two pulleys. The saw loop is closed by either brazing or by hooking the ends together. Band saws move quite fast at about six thousand feet per minute and at this time were powered by water or steam. It is possible that early saws were powered by horses, horses certainly were used in shingle making. A band saw could not cut sharp curves, so it is probable that both band saws and jig saws were used on the more complex patterns. In any case the boards would have had to have been finished by hand in most cases, always by hand if there were bevelled edges or pieces of applied wood or carved wood.

There must have been some improvements in jig sawing in the late 1870's as narrow pierced patterns became popular on exterior woodwork as well as on furniture. Spools or small pieces of turned wood became popular in the 1880's, but by this date barge boards were in devolution and spoolwork was used in the triangular peaks of gables and in the verandahs.

The earliest timber saw was the pit saw, a two-handled saw with one man standing on the adzed log while another worked below getting the sawdust in his eyes. With the introduction of water power the earliest saw mills used an up and down or re-ciprocating muley blade to cut logs into boards, but they were crude instruments. The circular or buzz saw was not common in Upper Canada till after 1840. Hand tools had developed over the centuries if not the milennia to a great sophistication. M. Pal-lardy quotes from an inventory of 1730 in Quebec which included a scroll saw and a tenon saw. The system of turning wood on a revolving lathe was known to the Ancient Egyptians.

During the heyday of the barge boards (1840-1870) white paint was far less in evidence than it was before and after these de-cades. Farm houses had to be congruent with their sites and their surroundings, rather than be the stark white-boarded and con-trasting impositions on the wilderness landscape of an earlier day. Southern Ontario had become a little tamed by 1840. In the neo-classic decade (1815-1835) light stone colour and pale grey blue walls were common with white exterior trim and cornice. In the romantic decade (1840-1850) exterior colours were quieter and drab. The barge boards seldom appeared on gables in colours greatly contrasting with those of the wall. As a typical example the *Canada Farmer* of May 16, 1867, recommended that the exterior walls of a frame house, which they sketched, should be painted a warm stone tint. The rest of the woodwork which in-cluded the barge boards was to be painted "a warm drab colour", except for the roof which was to be painted green. In one of Downing's books he shows a page of tints, each done painstakingly I think by hand in water colour. It is curious that the finial ironwork on the roof of the *Canada Farmer* house of 1867 was recommended to be painted "blue tipped with gold".

By the 1890's the sawings and turnings had run their course and society became sickened with profusion, and wood was getting scarcer. By 1900 we had a Georgian Revival, and if barge boards lingered on they served as functional boards at the junction of the gable wall with the roof, back there again to keep the rain and starlings out. In the 1920's we got an architect's revival of the English manor house often referred to as stock brokers' Tudor, but this was not a folk art.

It may be asked if all this evolutionary process did not go on elsewhere in North America. It did, especially in the U.S.A. after the American Civil War, but while New York State, Ontario's nearest U.S. neighbour, was in the throes of the Greek Revival before that war, Ontario was not. Also, in earlier settled areas where the classical tradition was solid, such as Montreal and Halifax, the bedecked Gothic had less impact. This was so in Kingston and Brockville as well. It had less support in Quebec. There are barge boards in every State and every Province. They are curiously scarce in England where they began. In many States and Provinces and English counties there are possibly architecturally superior examples, nevertheless in my opinion Ontario is very rich indeed in vernacular barge boards, which are, in design, geometric, floral, lineal, Gothic, Greek, Norman, Roman, Variegated, Admixed and Pot Pourri.

Perhaps they are not fine art nor even good architecture, but they are undoubtedly a folk art which does not have to be anything more than an exuberant expression of popular fancy. This is what this book will try to portray – an exuberant expression of popular fancy in Ontario.

I believe the right question to ask, respecting all ornament, is simply this: "Was it done with enjoyment – was the carver happy while he was about it?"

John Ruskin

Barge boards were first attached to gables on Ontario buildings by architects trained in the modern romantic manner of the late 1830's. As befits the educated professional these boards were designed with respectful regard for the detail found on European medieval buildings. But with white pine boards eighteen inches wide available in North America and with the Victorian arbiter of taste John Ruskin saying that craftsmen should be happy in their work we were not far into the 1840's before architects got away from the Fifteenth Century – quite a long way away. After that the humblest carpenter-builder could indulge himself in a licence never allowed him in the classical styles and legitimately be "happy while he was about it". At first they managed to keep to variations of Gothic designs but the variations gradually gave way to originality. "All good things which exist are the fruits of originality," said J. Stuart Mill and he was as Victorian as Ruskin. This section of photographs illustrates boards which are Gothic or at least of medieval inspiration.

Oakville

Burlington

near Georgetown

Brockville

near Colborne

near Carluke

Hamilton

North Ridge (near Essex)

Meadowvale

Toronto

Oakville

Dixie Rd. north of Mississauga

near Bell's Corners

near Manilla

near Georgetown

near Carluke

near Carluke

near Georgetown

near Ballinafad

St. Mary's

Orwell

Markham

Schomberg

near Nell's Corners

near Nell`s Corners

Oakville

People must not do things for fun. We are not here for fun.
There is no reference to fun in any Act of Parliament.

Sir A. P. Herbert

There is no reference to fun in the British North America Act either. Canadians are a fine hang-dog serious people and it is therefore surprising to find a section of this book on gables entitled Whimsy. Gothic style barge boards were still popular through the 1860's, especially with architects, but the carpenter-builder was beginning to feel no moral compulsion to rely on the Middle Ages for his inspiration.

No doubt if this book were a scholarly thesis its authors would have put gables into categories for a better comprehension. First there would be *Proper Gothic*. Then there would be *Improper Gothic*. Designs for both these would be based on window tracery, Tudor decorative bands, and structural elements such as hammer beam trusses and pendants hanging from Gothic stone vaults. Then there would be the *Eclectic* category, a little Greek here and there among Baroque cartouches all mixed in with vaguely floral or vaguely Gothic openwork. Then there would be a scholarly synonym for *Fun* with designs based on chain links, hearts, tulips, even hands. The final category would be a suitable rephrasing of *Inside Outside*. It would be indicated that Gable designs in this category were based on what was going on structurally inside the gable, collar ties, purlins and king-post trusses.

Mono Mills

Tillsonburg

Tillsonburg

Sunderland

Aylmer

Prescott

Mallorytown

Courtland

Oakville

St. Mary's

Frome

Schomberg

near Lynden

Streetsville

Aylmer

Burlington

Claude

Markham

Hamilton

Ottawa

Jarvis   *near Palmerston*

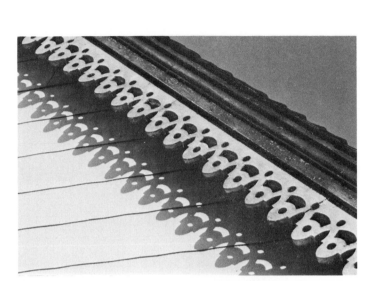

near Kintore

near Thamesford

Kingsville

Milton

near Mississauga

near Kintore

near Thamesford

Kingsville

near Mississauga

Milton

near Hillsburgh

Paris

near Cobourg

near Oakville

near Mono Mills

near Nobleton

Our father Adam sat under the tree and scratched with a
stick in the mould;
And the first rude sketch the world had seen was a joy to
his mighty heart,
Till the Devil whispered behind the leaves "It's pretty but
is it art?"

Rudyard Kipling

By the mid-1870's the Gothic Revival style for the vernacular house was out of date. The Italianate or Bracketed style and the imported French Empire style of Napoleon III with its Mansard roofs had surpassed the Gothic in popularity. Barge boards were in devolution. This devolution had begun when builders started on the category of gable previously described as "Inside Outside", with king-post trusses and collar ties expressed externally. These concentrated interest on the upper parts or the peaks of gables.

The history of most architectural styles is first Construction, then Ornamented Construction and then Constructed Ornament. This section of photographs entitled Peaks shows a lot of constructed ornament to which has been applied the pejorative word Gingerbread. Barge boards and eaves boards were still about in the 1880's and 1890's but they took second place to what was being constructed in the triangular peaks of gables. Gingerbread was cooked onto U.S. gables and facades with greater profusion than in Canada but there was some here. Its excessive fretwork, and spools, and fish scale shingles, and whittled brackets undoubtedly display forcefulness, but "is it art?" Each generation has its own taste. "You should never say it is not good. You should say you do not like it; then you know you are perfectly safe," said the American painter Whistler in 1888.

Holstein

Shelburne

School house: Rosemont

Milton

Hamilton

Nobleton

Waterdown

Burlington

Kingston

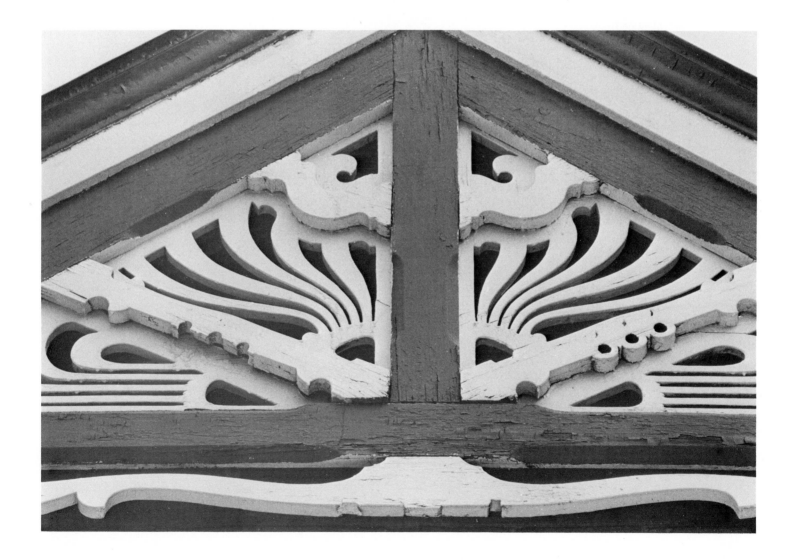

Kingston

Oakville

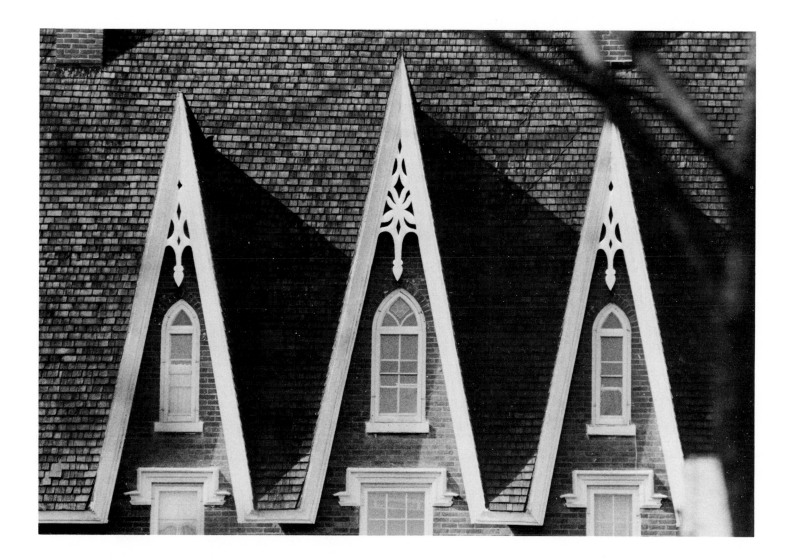

Bond Head

Shelburne

Tillsonburg

Milton

Alliston

Burlington

near Clappison`s Corners

Oakville

Paris

Caledonia

Milton

Tillsonburg

Hillsburgh

Morrisburg

Alliston

Line drawings by Anthony Adamson

*The painting "The Last of England"
by Ford Maddox Brown is reproduced
courtesy of the Birmingham Art Gallery,
England*

*The water-colour of York, Upper
Canada, 1804, by Elizabeth Frances Hale
is reproduced courtesy of the Public
Archives of Canada*